PROUD MOMENTS

INDIAN COUNTRY

You are about to enter
Indian country!

A land hidden
In history, tradition
And time honored custom.

Tread lightly among the people
Who dwell within its boundaries;
They welcome your arrival
But can see through false masks.

Watch out
That signs of poverty
Do not blind your perception
Of a proud people.

Forsake
Thoughts of trespassing
Where traditions are private;
Spirits guard sacred places.

Shed your judgments
And look
For beauty and goodness;
You will find it.

Grasp hospitality when given;
can hang
On your heart, forever.

You may now enter
Indian country!

PROUD MOMENTS

GENERATION TO GENERATION

Howard Rainer

Beautiful America Publishing Co.

Published by Beautiful America Publishing Company
9725 S.W. Commerce Circle
Wilsonville, Oregon 97070
©Copyright 1991 by Howard Rainer

Library of Congress Cataloging in Publication Data

Rainer, Howard
  Proud Moments.

  1. Indians of North America--Portraits. I. Title.
E89.R3   1988   970.004'97   88-16795
ISBN 0-89802-648-2

To Our Children

Editor, Design and Production: Carla Laurent

Special Adviser: Kristina Kennann

Printing: Korea

First Edition: Fall 1988

Second Edition: Spring 1994

CONTENTS

FOREWORD

This is an unusual, compelling book on contemporary Native Americans by Howard Rainer, a member of Taos Pueblo in northern New Mexico. But it comes from the mind and heart of all Indian America—that vast ethnic domain once stretching unbroken from Peru and Bolivia, through Guatemala and Mexico, into the American Southwest. It still exists in the United States as small islands in the sea of predominant Anglo culture.

Throughout pre-Columbian times all the great Indian civilizations were united, not politically, but by reverence for their common Mother Earth, and by the belief that all living bodies were interconnected in one universal body of all Creation.

The tribes in the United States have suffered genocide, decimation, and removal from their homelands to government reservations. The Cherokee 'Trail of Tears" and the Navajo "Long Walk" to captivity are outstanding examples. Yet the people have endured, passing on their pride of ancestry and their spiritual heritage from generation to generation.

Howard Rainer's book contains no reference to this unhappy past. He is concerned with the Native Americans of today and their hopes for the future. His photographs were taken as he traveled throughout the country, from one reservation to another. Most of the individuals photographed are in their workday clothes, old people and young people, men, women and children. Many of them are poor and may be discouraged, like we all are, by the rumbling advance of the technological Juggernaut of Progress into their lives. But as Rainer talks to them behind his camera, reminding them of who they are, their faces light up with a renewed sense of pride and dignity.

Here too are landscape shots of mountains, plains and desert, and the boundless sky, the world of nature with which they are so intimately related. A few short poems by Rainer emphasizes the spiritual ecology they practice.

The whole thrust of his book is to show the commonality of their human spirit. For this reason the names of the individuals and their tribes are not given.

The publisher of *Proud Moments* has given it a dignity of format and purity of form, as shown by its organically arranged contents. It also has been extremely fortunate in having as editor, Carla Laurent, who intuitively apperceives the fundamental values of Native American culture.

"Native American heritage", she writes, "is that of a close relationship with nature, with the family, being connected with the whole. From this experience comes a sense of order, a common spirit as manifested in the human sense of pride and dignity".

Their holistic world-outlook and "sense of order" to which she refers are of growing significance to us all today in this tragic time of world distress. It may not be out of place to make a few comments about them.

The religious Native American culture and that of our materialistic Anglo culture have been opposed since they first met. For three centuries science imposed upon Western civilization the Newtonian "clockwork universe" concept of isolated, disconnected parts operating independently. In contrast, the Native American concept was that every living part—star, earth, man, plant, insect—was interconnected, forming a universal whole.

Today theoretical science is developing a new picture of reality that is surprisingly like that of Native Americans. One of its leading spokesmen is Dr. David Bohm, a former associate of Einstein, and who is regarded as the world's most renowned theoretical physicist. In his advanced view he asserts that physical matter (which is energy informed with consciousness) is constantly enfolded into a unity where nothing is separate from the whole. All particles in the universe, from electrons to stars and galaxies, are connected to all others in what he calls an "implicate order".

In this "implicate order" the cosmic image of the entire universe is reflected in each of its parts.

Moreover, he asserts that we human beings, as parts of the whole, also embody its all-pervading consciousness in our own now-limited human consciousness.

To change the world, he insists, we must change our way of thinking—fragmenting the world into quarreling and destructive parts, races, nations, religions, communities. Only by thinking from the whole to the parts, instead of the parts, can we bring peace and order to the world.

It seems, then, that the new, modern world-view is converging with the ancient world-view held by Native Americans. Their images and languages are different, but their meaning is the same. While our Anglo view has not been generally accepted, there are thousands of people throughout the world who are seeing life in larger perspective.

This is why these photographs in *Proud Moments*, why Native Americans are so important. Their holographic vision of unity and harmony has long been translated into their daily lives, and is reflected by their pride and dignity. We have much to learn from them as we both face the future.

Frank Waters

INTRODUCTION

"We are going to teach you who you are. Then when you go out into the world, it will live inside you."

This was spoken by my wise grandparents who lived in the secluded village of Taos Pueblo near the Sangre de Cristo Mountains in northern New Mexico.

Their daily example and patient instructions imbued within me a reverence for Pueblo life. Many seasonal traditions and customs in our village prepared us for manhood. Both grandparents taught me the importance of community responsibility. They admonished me to actively take part in tribal ceremonies, village dances and designated clan assignments.

My grandfather, a respected political and religious leader of the Taos Pueblo Tribe, played an important role as a spokesman and advocate for Pueblo rights.

My father followed my grandfather's footsteps. My grandfather counseled my father to sacrifice the security of Pueblo life, and to attain a college education from the University of Redlands and the University of Southern California. Years later, my father became a respected Indian educator. But more important, was a national Indian leader who worked to protect and secure Indian rights.

He also developed a national Indian scholarship organization to financially aid Indian men and women in obtaining their Masters and Doctorate degrees. My father's scholarship efforts helped over 2,300 Native American men and women to obtain their post-graduate degrees. As All-Indian Pueblo Council chairman, my father was an active voice for Indian rights in New Mexico. His daring fight won the right to vote in state and local elections for the Pueblo Indians.

I am indebted to these two men. They inspired me to pursue the challenging work of promoting educational opportunities among Indian people throughout North America. Their years of unselfish service taught another family generation the value of contributing to society and our people.

Sharing and contributing towards mankind's betterment is important. But the strength and spirit to accomplish this came from the quiet and gentle teachings of my mother and grandmother. I was fortunate to have these two women influence my life, preparing me to accept and appreciate spiritual values. Their ways centered on recognizing the power of the Great Creator God and His love for our people on this earth.

My grandmother saying her nightly prayers by kerosene lamp left a profound impression on me. A worthy person must communicate with and rely upon the One who created us.

Our people and family called my grandmother "the light". They recognized her good spirit and the radiance she shared with those people she loved.

My mother took great care to insure that my brother, sister, and I have spiritual roots and religious values. My highest tribute to this stately woman is to incorporate her spiritual examples into my family.

Like most Indian people, the day comes, however traumatic, when cultural transition must take place. Indian people regardless of age or tribe, travel an uneven road trying to balance their sense of belonging, self-identity, and well-being between two conflicting worlds.

As a little boy, it was a devastating experience going from a reservation day school to a public school three miles away from my village. However, I'm sure that it prepared me for my destined work with Indian youth across America and Canada.

There were many dark years of adjustment and failure. But, I learned the great lessons of acceptance and rejection by teachers, apprehensive adjustment with other races, confusion of conflicting cultural values, and the hidden strength to conquer self-doubt.

I am most grateful for all the experiences in obtaining a formal non-Indian education. I also recognize life's teachings that gave me an unique insight and a broader dimension to reaching out to other Indian people. I've also promoted education among others that relate to my past school experiences. Hopefully, I can encourage them to rise above their rejection and failures.

Proud Moments is a most appropriate title for this book. Having met stately Indian men, such as the late Mr. William Minthorn, Umatilla Tribe, Pendleton, Oregon, provided the inspiration and will to create such a book. Meeting him and his dear wife, Vivian, left a fond, memorable impression upon me. It rekindled that fire and pride of being an American Indian!

I dedicate this book and my photographic quest to these proud people. These dignified people have shared, somewhat cautiously, their goodness, their dreams and visions, and some of their pain.

Without their trust and permission to look into their eyes and see what is in their hearts, this book would still be only a dream.

Howard Rainer

ANCESTORS SPEAK

"Is not the sky a father
   and the earth a mother,
   and are not all living things
   with feet or wings or roots their children?"

FATHER SKY

MOTHER EARTH

"Each part of the earth is sacred to my people.

Every shining pineneedle,
every light mist in the dark woods,
every clearing...

and every humming insect...

*is sacred in the memory
and experiences of my people...*

*We are a part of the earth
and it is a part of us.*

The fragrant flowers are our sisters;

the deer, ... and the mighty eagle are...
our brothers.

The rocky peaks,
the fertile meadows,

... all things are connected
like the blood that unites a family..."

Chief Seattle   1887

PROUD MOMENTS

...Proud Heritage

PROUD MOMENTS

The young
are the sunrise of our people.

Look into their faces;
there is something strong
burning in their eyes.

Many great thoughts
will come from their curious minds.

Many will hear the whispers
of noble chiefs
speaking of courage in their ears.

Some will heed the counsel
and their paths
will be filled with proud moments.

Others will see the visions
and dreams
granted to those with good spirits.

This is the dawning
for a people
who have waited for this generation.

They are ready
to be led for a season;
then we will see them in front
leading with power from above.

Many proud moments are ahead!

"Our religion is the traditions of our ancestors --
   the dreams of our old men,
   given them in the solemn hours of night
   by the Great Spirit...
   and is written in the hearts of our people."

Chief Seattle 1855

THE ELDERS

THE WISE OWL

I am
the wise owl of my tribe.

I sit with watchful eyes,
witnessing the young wanting
to change our ways.

My ears
are in tune with voices from the past.

Inside my mind,
I can recite all the songs and secrets
tied to traditions
before many were born.

I sit in my nest,
watching,
waiting for someone
sincere to ask me who we are.

I will not speak unless spoken to.
I will not tell
until they have proven themselves.
I will not give counsel if no one cares.

A wise owl must be respected!

I DARE YOU

I dare you
to capture my spirit!

I am not afraid;
I am who I am.

You may take my picture;
but that is all.

My eyes warn you.

What is inside
must remain
until you
become my friend.
Until then,
I dare you.

GREETER

He stood at the entrance
of our reservation
and welcomed me home.

My heart felt his embrace.

He was the remaining sentry
still keeping watch
without sadness.

A Greeter at the gate.

NEVER ALONE

When I feel lost
and darkness surrounds my heart,
I sing grandfather's song,
and ancestors dance all around me.

An Indian
is never alone!

OLD LOVE

Old love is good.

Children
have come and gone,
grandchildren
now carry our name.

Dark days
have challenged our courage;
we are still here.

Hard times
have tested our faith,
we look at each other
still the same.

Old love is good!

GRANDMOTHER

Grandmother making fry bread; she smiles,
chopping wood; she teaches,
holding grandchildren; she tells the stories
of my people; she smiles;
she is the joy and warmth of my people.
I love her!

SUNDOWNS

*We have spent
many sundowns together.*

*I have held you
in my lap
so these moments
would bind us forever.*

*My tired hands
have wiped your tears away;
but who will dry mine
when you are gone?*

*Soon,
my lap will be empty,
and sundowns
will be watched alone.*

*Let us sit now
together in silence
so that when you become a woman,
memories will tie our horizons
forever.*

HEAR MY WORDS

Hear my words
and listen with your heart.

My season is nearing the end.

I have walked with all
of your grandfathers
and they have left me behind.

If they were here,
they would give you the same counsel
from their lips.

Listen to your spirit.
Share your gifts and
carry the name of your forefathers.
We are a part of you.

Then someday,
we will meet again.

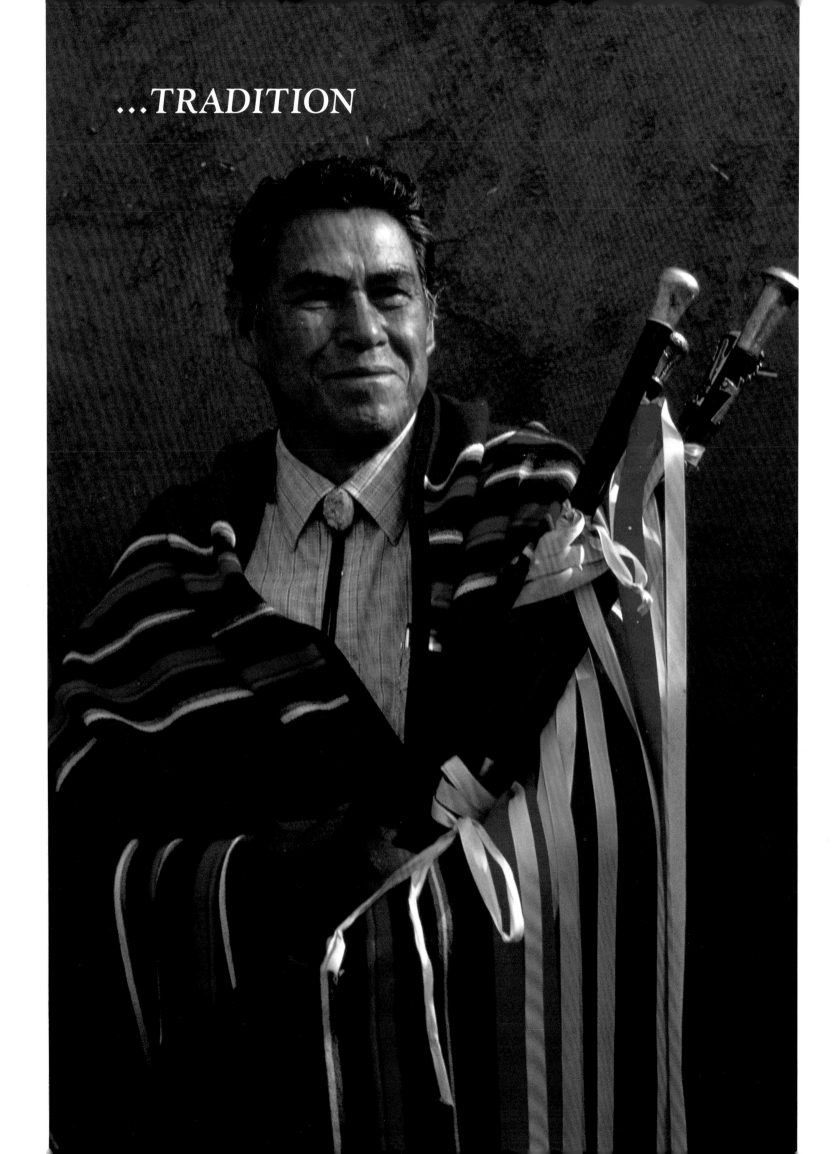

...TRADITION

"The Great Tellings"

THE STORYTELLER

FIRST FALL

Many winters ago
timeless traditions
surrounded the first snow
at Taos Pueblo.

The echoes of orders shouted
from the roof tops
to usher a call
to Pueblo men;
come together
and shovel the first fall.

The thump from metal axes
splitting pitchy pine and red cedar
for the evenfall fires.

Wonderment in watching
blankets of white snow
gently cover dwellings
that defied the elements,
just like the old people.

It was just winters ago
I heard the whispers of grandmother
encouraging silence
as a sign of reverence
in her house.

The Tiwa
believed in a quiet season;
a time of stillness
to not awaken mother earth;
for she would need her strength
for the budding of spring.

...HARMONY

*needs to be maintained
between this world
and the spiritual one...*

Offerings...

...Thanksgiving

CRAFTSMEN

We create beautiful things because
beauty is what we see.
We use our hands that are guided by
good thoughts.
What we make holds our feelings.
The Creator has given us special gifts,
we share them with you.

PASSING ON...

GENERATION TO GENERATION

HUMMING BIRDS

Humming birds hovering
Close to their grandpa.

Fluttering their wings of admiration,
They circle,
Teasing and taunting for his attention.

Their presence pure joy,
Grandfather's spirit dancing
As they nudge at him,
Seeking the saged nectar.

With the tender touch of the beak
They express their elation,
Celebrating in the union for the moment.

Suddenly they dart away
Disappearing into womanhood;
Memories of granddaughters
The spring of his thoughts forever.

One touch of a tiny hand
plants the seeds of love
and teaches hard men
its meaning.

A little one's coo
caresses the heart
of the mother.

Little spirits
Images of God.

THE CHILDREN

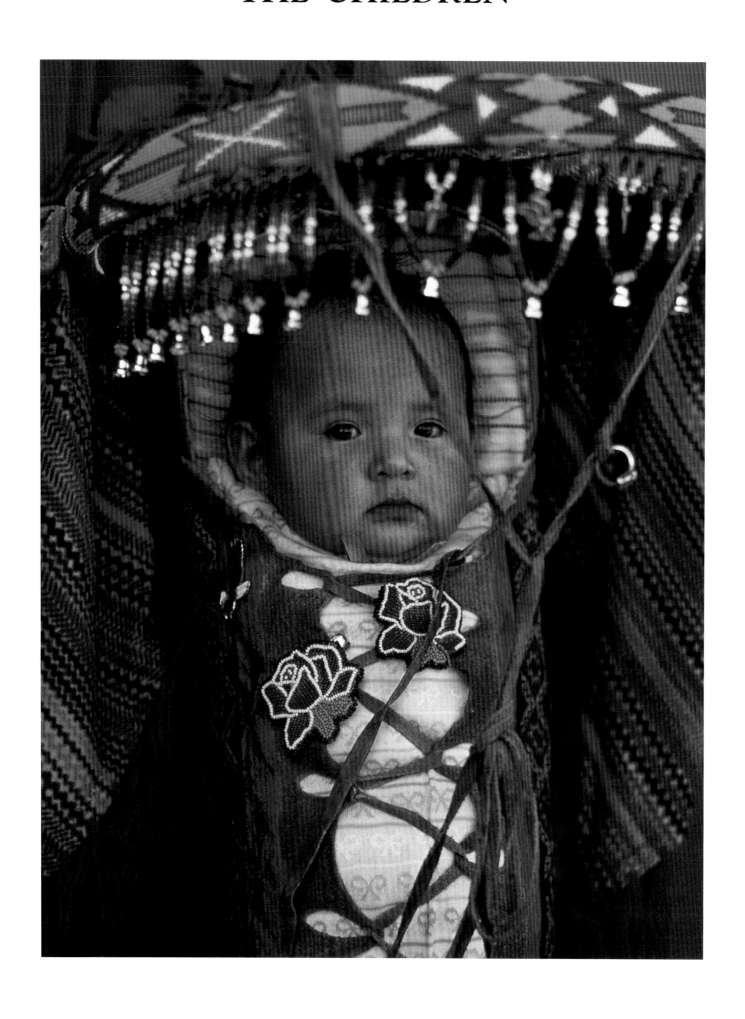

I AM YOUNG

My ears hear promise,
my mind is power,
my eyes see dreams.
My thoughts are high,
my body is strong,
I am beautiful.
I am young!

LITTLE SPIRIT

When our eyes meet
my heart
flutters like the humming bird.

Happiness
dances all around you.

Little spirit…
a mother's song forever.

MOTHER EAGLE

I saw
the mother of eagles
perched above
a crowd of hundreds.

Her majesty
motioned my spirit
for a closer look.

Dignity
surrounded her
and introduced her presence.

Eaglets of all ages
fluttered around her,
seeking her strength and wisdom.

Her fearless face
told everything.
Here before me stood
the Eagle among eagles.

FROM AGE TO AGE

I AM

I am
Indian woman.

The giver of life
to warriors, chiefs
and generations to come.

FUTURE DREAMS...

AND SONGS

FLUTE MAKER

My fingers
gently press the holes
across the flute
asking for a song
to flow forth.

My ears
wait to hear the echos
from inside
the hollow center,
from voices
of flute makers since gone.

A pleasant sound
rushes out,
filling my mind with good thoughts.

My heart tells me,
another
once played this song.

...the eagle feather here is for
...the thoughts of men
 that should rise high
 as eagles do.

Black Elk 1931

WHERE DID I COME FROM?

Look up in the sky,
where eagles look like humming birds.
Look beyond the clouds,
where stars look like tiny fires.
Look and ask:
Who created Indian?
Who created me?
Some call him Watonka,
some call him Creator,
others call him Great Spirit.
I call him God.
The Father of heaven and of my earth.

SETTING SUN

The setting sun
cast its final light
on the rolling hills of the Badlands.

Indian Summer
was bidding her farewell
and the chilly winds blew forth
a subtle warning-
the bleakness of winter
was at hand.

Strange sounds whispered
through the valleys and grasslands.

It was the eerie call
of a coyote
crying out in his native tongue.

I watched him
standing with gaze intent,
looking in desperation
for someone.

My ears heard his howling
making my heart weep.

I stood there wondering
who was he calling out to;

I've been that coyote
a thousand times!

EPILOGUE

MANKIND

I'll be this
and you'll be that.
I'll be black,
and you'll be white—
and red will be alright.
And when this is
all over,
we'll be buried,
separate…but equal.

Dedicated to my Father,
John C. Rainer

ACKNOWLEDGEMENTS

The author is grateful for permission to use excerpts from the following publications:

Black Elk Speaks by John G. Neihardt, copyright Neihardt 1932, 1959, published by The University of Nebraska Press and Simon & Schuster Pocket Books.

Touch the Earth by T.C. McLuhan, copyright T.C. McLuhan 1971. Reprinted by permission of E.P. Dutton, a division of NAL Penguin Inc.

American Indian Basketry edited and published by John M. Gogol, copyright American Indian Basketry and Other Native Arts December 30, 1984.

SPEAK FOR ME

Let my camera
speak for me.

Let these photographs be
a lasting tribute
to the people I love!